DOCUMENT EXERCISE WORKBOOK FOR
VOLUME I: TO 1800
WORLD HISTORY

DOCUMENT EXERCISE WORKBOOK FOR
VOLUME I: TO 1800
WORLD HISTORY

WILLIAM J. DUIKER
PENNSYLVANIA STATE UNIVERSITY

JACKSON J. SPIELVOGEL
PENNSYLVANIA STATE UNIVERSITY

PREPARED BY
DONNA VAN RAAPHORST
CUYAHOGA COMMUNITY COLLEGE

West/Wadsworth
I(T)P® An International Thomson Publishing Company

Belmont, CA • Albany, NY • Bonn • Boston • Cincinnati • Detroit • Johannesburg • London
Madrid • Melbourne • Mexico City • New York • Paris • Singapore • Tokyo • Toronto • Washington

Senior Developmental Editor: Sharon Adams Poore
Print Buyer: Stacey Weinberger
Project Editor: Howard Severson

ISBN 0-534-53124-5

For Barbara - my way station gift
until Alcatraz

Contents

Vol. I

Foreword

To The Student

To The Instructor

Foreword

The genesis of this work has been twenty some years of classroom instruction. Throughout this time period my students have been my best teachers and this book is a reflection of what has been most successful with them.

Many individuals helped to make these volumes possible especially those at West Educational Publishing.

Equally supportive were numerous individuals on the Western Campus of Cuyahoga Community College. Of special note are my Provost, Mr. Ronald M. Sobel, my departmental colleague, Ms. Mary Hovanec, my word processor, Ms. Elizabeth Russin, and Ms. Mikki Shackelton, a former student. Last but not least I am particularly grateful to my trusted and true friend Mary Kay Howard of John Carroll University for our numerous "brainstorming sessions." Without their assistance, aid, and cooperation this work would not have been possible.

To The Student

This supplement was written with you in mind. Specifically, it was designed to complement the textbook you are reading in your world history course. This small volume includes some documents that you will find in your text and several that are not.

The method of organization is chronological and the exercises that accompany the documents will progress from the relatively simple to the far more complex. The documents reflect the wide range of materials historians use in attempting to reconstruct the past. If you begin using this supplement when your coursework commences and continue to use it throughout the duration of your survey study of World History, you will develop a better understanding of historical source materials and of how historians study history.

To The Instructor

This slim volume was written to accompany a world history course and these exercises should be useful as a supplement to any text.

The materials within are arranged in a typical chronological fashion, but this book attempts to be more than simply another collection of documents. It endeavors to engage the student in a study of the past through a series of carefully constructed exercises using primary sources. These exercises are intended to develop thinking skills appropriate to the study of history. As such, they progress from those relatively simple in nature to those far more complex. More importantly, the exercises are ultimately aimed, as Russel H. Hvolbek has aptly written, for "the primary purpose of teaching history and the humanities (which) is to make students more aware of how their lives connect to the past human experience." This objective cannot be achieved by simply acquiring a body of knowledge. Students will come much closer to this goal if they learn how to seek out information and if they learn how to use this information. Hvolbek informs us that this is our ultimate responsibility in reevaluating how we teach our discipline with the provocative title of his essay--"History and Humanities: Teaching as Destructive of Certainty." (AHA Perspectives, January, 1991)

Chapter I
The Nature of History

Before you read this important introductory chapter, write your definition of history on a piece of paper and then put your response aside. When you have finished reading this chapter, examine anew your original thoughts. Compare the differences you find. Think about these differences.

This simple exercise is intended to challenge your presumptions about history. History is not what many of you think it to be. It is not the acquisition of a body of information--names, dates, places, events--simply to be memorized and then shortly forgotten. History is much more. History is far more difficult, far more thought-provoking, far more profound, far more exciting, and more important, far more meaningful to your lives. In fact, one could argue that it is the most important subject you will ever study. When examined and understood properly, history provides us with insights into the fundamental questions that have always concerned humanity beginning with who am I and why am I here? When you understand history you will have become an informed, literate, insightful, thinking human being.

Understood in this way, history would be classified as part of a larger group of disciplines identified as the humanities. An even more thoughtful way to think of history, along with the other humanities, is as the Report of the Colloquium on the Humanities and the American People, has done:

> We identify them, rather, with certain ways of thinking--of inquiring, evaluating, judging, finding, and articulating meaning . . . . They are taken together, the necessary resources of a reflective approach to life. The value of a reflective approach can be best appreciated by considering the alternative: a life unilluminated by imagination, uninformed by history, unguided by reasoning--in short, the "unexamined life" that Socrates described as not worth living . . . .(1)

In order that these statements reflect more than grandiloquent expressions of a historian about their chosen discipline, three important questions must be addressed. They are the following: What is history?; How does the historian proceed?; and, What is history for?

A logical place to turn in your attempt to answer the first question, "What is history?," would be a dictionary of word origins or a book of word histories. In so doing you are examining the etymology of the word--its history or its origins. Etymologically, then, history simply denotes "knowledge." This should be interesting for you to discover because the most simplistic understanding of history is often that it is the accumulation of information. To arrive at the more complex aspects of our word, a more specific modern meaning must be uncovered.

The modern story (frequently another common definition of history) begins with the Greek word histor, meaning "learned man." In turn, histor is a descendant of the Indo-European word wid, which is defined as to "know" or "see." This led to the English word wit and the Latin word videre, meaning "see." From histor the word historia evolved and, for you, its meaning is of utmost significance. The definition of historia is "knowledge obtained by inquiring, or a written account of one's inquiries."(2) History, then is a process of inquiring. Specifically the historian, as well as the student of history, inquires into the past and records his or her findings.

Use of the word inquire says something important because it implies a process of asking questions that leads to an interpretation of the evidence. A process is doing and that is the essence of what this small book is trying to teach you--how to <u>do</u> history rather than be a passive recipient of information.(3) In order to do history, you must learn how to ask good questions. Obviously the historian (in this case you) proceeds by asking questions about things that happened in the past. Simple enough, right? Not really, not after you have thought about it momentarily.

Whether you realize it or not, some questions are not appropriate to the discipline of history. For example, you would not ask questions about the past failure of your compact disk player to work properly. Questions not germane to humans, their activities, their institutions, their culture, their economy are inappropriate for historical investigation. However, the main difficulty confronting historians isn't eliminating unimportant or unanswerable questions. It is, instead, choosing from among the important ones.

Generally speaking, the important questions historians ask of their evidence, called sources, are--the who; the why; the when; the where; and, most important of all, the so what? Reflect for a moment on this as you read the following ideas of the well-known Yale historian, Professor Robin W. Winks, on history and asking good questions:

> History is, fundamentally, applied common sense. History begins in the fascination of discreet fact. History is curiosity, a desire to poke and pry to get answers to questions. History is asking good questions. [But not all these questions will, or should, be answered--save one.] The most challenging question, a damaging question that should be asked of any lecturer who ever spelled out a theory, is to look them straight in the eye and say, "Yes, but so what?" It's a paralyzing question. It's soul-destroying. And yet the historian <u>must</u> be able to answer the question.(4)

Mention of sources has been made several times. Historical sources are found in a variety of forms and places. In fact, historical sources, evidence of the past, are everywhere around you. Here are some examples--letters, maps, photographs, cemeteries, reports, personal diaries, buildings, recordings. The list is all but endless, but most traditionally the historian works with written sources, which are commonly referred to as documents. A document is defined as "a thing existing here and now, of such a kind that the historian, by thinking about it, can get answers to the questions he asks about past events."(5)

Generally speaking, when the historian uses the word document, he or she means "primary source" material. This means a record of the actual words of someone who either participated or witnessed whatever is being described. Primary sources are one of two basic types of evidence the historian uses in reconstructing the past.

The other is referred to as a "secondary source." A secondary source is the interpretation of an individual who did not participate or witness whatever is being descibed, but who investigated the primary source(s), e.g., an historian.

If good questions need to be formulated in order to interpret your source materials, you also need to examine your evidence carefully for bias, for accuracy, for content. Suppose you were to write a biography of Winston Churchill. Would it be wise to rely only on funeral orations; family memoirs; the opinions of political opponents? Why not? In other words, as you evaluate your sources, you need to consider the circumstances under which they were written. What might have been the motive of the author? What was the relationship of the writer to the individual in question? What was the relationship of the author to the person, the place, the event, the time in question? One source needs to be checked against another to try and establish as full and as accurate a picture of the past as possible. As possible, or course, implies incomplete. Did you ever realize or consider this fact?

Think of it in terms of the philosophical issue of the forest and the tree. In that forest how many trees exist? How many of those trees can you actually observe? Even if you say one and you are standing under it, how many of its limbs can you observe, how many of its actual branches, and, how many of its leaves? When you consider this, you can perhaps begin to comprehend the true meaning of as possible and incomplete. The author Janet Malcolm expressed it beautifully when she wrote, "in a work of nonfiction we almost never know the truth of what happened. The ideal of unmediated reporting is regularly achieved only in fiction, where the writer faithfully reports on what is going on in his imagination . . . ."(6)

One final aspect concerning the question of how the historian proceeds needs to be addressed. That question concerns itself with the matter of organization--how are the source materials discovered about the past to be organized in such a way that significant information becomes apparent? Examination of this issue has demonstrated certain basic human activities that clearly stand out and answer basic questions. These activities fall into the following categories: political; economic; social; religious; scientific; cultural; and, intellectual. Some might also include technological and artistic. Remember these as you progress through the various exercises in this book and as you study and learn for your history course.

Almost fifty years ago now, R. G. Collingwood, a Professor of Philosophy at Oxford and a practicing historian, asked and answered the final question under consideration in this chapter: "What is history for?" Conceding it to be the most difficult and highly individualistic in nature, Collingwood nonetheless wrote,

> My answer is that history is 'for' human self-knowledge. It is generally thought to be of importance to man that he should know himself: where knowing himself means knowing not his merely personal peculiarities . . . but his nature as man. Knowing yourself means knowing first, what it is to be a man; secondly, knowing what it is to be the kind of man you are; and thirdly, knowing what it is to be the man you are and nobody else is. Knowing yourself means knowing what you can do; and since nobody knows what he can do until he tries, the only clue to what man can do is what man has done. The value of history, then, is that it teaches us what man has done and thus what man is.(7)

6

Endnotes

1. Merrill D. Peterson, <u>The Humanities and the American Promise</u>, Report of the Colloquium on the Humanities and the American People (Austin, Texas: Texas Committee for the Humanities, 1987), 2-3.

2. <u>Dictionary of Word Origins</u>, s.v. "history," and <u>The Merriam-Webster New Book of Word Histories</u>, s.v. "history."

3. Finlay McQuade, "What is <u>doing</u> a discipline?" (Waltham, MA: The College Board, n.d.).

4. "For Sleuth, History is Where He Finds It," <u>The Plain Dealer</u>, 11 February, 1990.

5. R. G. Collingwood, <u>The Idea of History</u> (New York: Oxford University Press, 1946; A Galaxy Book, 1956), 10.

6. Janet Malcolm, "The Silent Woman - III," <u>The New Yorker</u>, 23 & 30 August, 1993, 138.

7. Collingwood, <u>The Idea of History</u>, 10.

Chapter II
Applying the Basics to Historical Sources

Now that you have addressed the essentials and come to terms with a new understanding and appreciation of the complexities of history, you should be ready to actually try your hand at doing some history. In this chapter your exercises will deal with two types of source materials. Scholars of very early history frequently have to rely on other than strictly written materials like documents. It is important for you to understand how to use a variety of source materials even in your attempt to understand the modern world. Consider how many letters you have written lately? Do you keep a written diary?

Your first exercise will focus on a coin, what is commonly classified as an artifact. Coins have a history of their own; one that begins in the western part of Asia Minor in an early civilization called Lydia. Establishing a brief hegemony over Asia Minor from the middle of the 7th to the middle of the 6th century B.C., the Lydians are believed to have invented metallic coinage. Prior to this, jewelry was probably the closest thing to money.(1) Lydians are also responsible for establishing the first permanent retail shops and together these two important contributions to civilization played a role as catalyst in bringing about a commercial revolution helping to transform 6th century B.C. Greek civilization.

Let us suppose you find the coin pictured on the next page in the ruins of a very ancient civilization about which you know absolutely nothing. You are able to decifer the language for it is very similar to your own. However, you don't understand how this came to be. Study the coin carefully and then do the following:

1. List five to ten things you believe you can determine about this civilization.

2. Take your list and categorize it according to those most commonly used by historians to organize their information. Remember what they are?--political; economic; social; religious; scientific; cultural; and, intellectual.

Are you surprised by how much can be determined with one piece of evidence? Did you ever think of coins as an historical source? Actually, they are often invaluable to the historian. For instance, almost no records exist to inform us about the Parthian dynasty in 247 B.C. The Parthians were originally a nomadic people from central Asia, who at some point in history entered Iran (ancient Persia). Apparently they were at their peak of power about the end of the second century B.C. Tucked between two far greater powers--Rome to the west and China to the east--they were able to control at least a part of the great Silk Route and act as middlemen between their mightier neighbors. Inscriptions on coins and potsherds (pieces of broken earthen pots) have helped to corroborate the only other source materials available: the findings of archaeologists and subjective accounts of classical Greek and Roman texts.(2) Are you convinced?

Try working with a more conventional piece of historical evidence, an actual document and in this case a very famous early code of laws--the Code of Hammurabi. Much more can be found out about Hammurabi by reading and reviewing your textbook. As for the Code, it was cut in a diorite shaft nearly eight feet high and was discovered some time early in the 20th century by French archaeologists at a place called Susa, in modern-day Iran. Unknown persons had transported it there from Babylon.(3)

From this point on, whenever you are working with a document, always perform the following procedures:

- Have a dictionary by your side. You cannot understand a document if you do not understand the vocabulary.

- As you read through the document, circle all unfamiliar words and look them up in your dictionary.

- As you read through the document, look for the important ideas that relate to the question or questions you are seeking to answer (the who?; the why?; the when?; the where?; and the so what?). Underline them.

- Write these ideas out in your own words. In this way you will better understand them.

Remember these procedures as you make your way through the sections of the Code provided on the next few pages. Write and work on them as they are designed with that in mind.

DOCUMENT

The Code of Hammurabi

Prologue

When the lofty Anu, king of the Anunaki, and Enlil, lord of heaven and earth, who

determines the destinies of the land, committed the rule of all mankind to Marduk,

the first-born son of Ea, and made him great among the Igigi; when they pronounced the lofty name of Babylon, made it great among the quarters of the world and in its midst established for him an everlasting kingdom whose foundations were firm as heaven and earth--at that time Anu and Enlil named me Hammurabi, the exalted prince, the worshipper of the gods, to cause righteousness to prevail in the land, to destroy the wicked and the evil, to prevent the strong from plundering the weak, to go forth like the sun over the black-headed race, to enlighten the land and to further the welfare of the people . . . .

The ancient seed of royalty, the powerful king, the sun of Babylon, who caused light to go forth over the lands of Sumer and Akkad; the king who caused the four quarters of the world to render obedience; the favorite of Innanna am I. When Marduk sent me to rule the people and to bring help to the land, I established law and justice in the language of the land and promoted the welfare of the people.

The Laws

25. If a fire break out in a man's house and a man who goes to extinguish it cast his eye on the household property of the owner of the house, and take the household property of the owner of the house, that man shall be thrown into the fire.

26. If either an officer or a constable who is ordered to go on an errand of the king do not go . . . that officer or constable shall be put to death . . . .

42. If a man rent a field for cultivation and do not produce any grain in the field, because he has not performed the necessary work on the field they shall convict him, and he shall give to the owner of the field grain on the basis of the adjacent fields.

87. If he put out money at interest, for one shekel of silver he shall receive one-fifth of a shekel as interest.

128. If a man take a wife and do not draw up a contract with her, that woman is not a wife.

150. If a man make his wife a present of field, garden, house, and goods and deliver to her a sealed deed, after the death of her husband, her children may

not make any claim to her. The mother after her death may give them to her child who she loves, but to a brother she may not give them.

168. If a man set his face to disinherit his son and say to the judges, "I will disinherit my son," the judges shall inquire into his past, and if the son have not committed a crime sufficiently grave to cut him off from sonship, the father may not cut off his son from sonship.

196. If a man destroy the eye of another man, they shall destroy his eye.

197. If he break a man's bone, they shall break his bone.

198. If he destroy the eye of a common man or break a bone of a common man, he shall pay one mina of silver.

199. If he destroy the eye of a man's slave or break a bone of a man's slave, he shall pay one-half his price.

200. If a man knock out a tooth of a man of his own rank, they shall knock out his tooth.

201. If he knock out a tooth of a common man, he shall pay one-third mina of silver.

218. If a physician make a deep incision upon a man with his bronze lancet and cause the man's death, or operate on the eye socket of a man with his bronze lancet and destroy the man's eye, they shall cut off his hand.

229. If a builder erect a house for a man and do not make its construction firm, and the house which he built collapse and cause the death of the owner of the house, that builder shall be put to death.(4)

QUESTIONS

Now that you have read the document and followed the preceding steps, answer the three questions below:

1. Apply the categories used by the historian to organize information--what in the document is political history; economic history; social history; and so forth. For purposes of simplification, place abbreviations after appropriate sentences or statements in the Prologue and after each law in question eg. (p) political, (soc) social, (sci) scientific. Write directly in your workbook.

2. Upon completion of your categorization, write a short paragraph describing what you believe life in Hammurabi's Mesopotamia was like. Use as many of the categories as you can to provide as complete a picture of this society as you can.

3. Examine your results. Think about what you have done. Do you have a better understanding of history and what the historian does after completing this exercise?

14

Endnotes

1. Margaret Oliphant, <u>The Atlas of the Ancient World: Charting the Great Civilizations of the Past</u> (New York: Simon & Shuster, 1992), 67-69.

2. <u>Ibid</u>., 76.

3. George H. Knoles and Rixford K. Snyder, ed., <u>Readings In Western Civilization</u>, 3rd ed. (Chicago: J. B. Lippincott Company, 1960), 3.

4. Louis Cohn-Haft, ed., <u>Source Readings in Ancient History</u>, Vol. I: <u>The Ancient Near East and Greece</u> (New York: Macmillan Publishing Company, 1965), 81-84; 86; 89; 91; 93; 96-98; 102.

Chapter III
A Basic Historical Skill - Selection

At this point in your study, you should have begun to develop a deeper appreciation of the complexity of history and the focus of your course of study--civilizations of the world. Probably you have had a little prior exposure to the development of those civilized communities that emerged in the river basins of the Tigris, Euphrates, and Nile. Most likely fewer of you have learned about equally significant centers of civilization in other parts of Africa or the Yellow and Indus River regions.

This chapter will focus on one of those less often studied centers of development, the Indus, by engaging in a most fundamental historical skill, the skill of selection. Consider the fact that a process of selection takes place in virtually all human activity. Why do you choose to do one thing rather than another? How did you go about deciding to take this history course and not one that focused on the United States? What thinking processes did the authors of your text use in deciding what information to include in the chapter about early India? What thinking processes determined the information that would be excluded from this same chapter?

Think about this very carefully considering text statements like the following:

"India, then, is a land of diversity. This diversity is evident in its languages and cultures as well as in its physical characteristics."

"In its size and diversity, India seems more like a continent than a single country."(1)

Reflect on this again in light of a question you may well have asked yourself when preparing for an examination--How do I decide what is important enough to be on my exam?

What, then, is historical selection? Consider what should take place. You will enter into a dialogue with your sources--"a process by which the mind selects ever more accurately the sources and at the same time refines the questions it needs to ask the sources."(2)

Think about it anew as you ponder the following problem relating to the Macedonian, Alexander the Great, whose empire extended as far eastward as the Indus River Valley. Sometime in June, 323 B.C., Alexander, the man who wished to Hellenize the world, died. In that last year of his life, literally thousands upon thousands of things happened to him. Why have historians chosen to record so few of them?(3)

Remembering what you have thought about, read the passage from the famous Indian epic, the Mahabharata, and answer the questions that follow it.

DOCUMENT

The Mahabharata

Yudhisthira said: "This word 'king' [raja] is so very current in this world, O Bharata;

how has it originated? Tell me that O grandfather."

Bhishma said: "Certainly, O best among men, do you listen to everything in its entirety--how kingship originated first during the golden age [krtayuga]. Neither kingship nor king was there in the beginning, neither scepter [danda] nor the bearer of a scepter. All people protected one another by means of righteous conduct, O Bharata, men eventually fell into a state of spiritual lassitude.

Then delusion overcame them. Men were thus overpowered by infatuation, O leader of men, on account of the delusion of understanding; their sense of righteous conduct was lost. When understanding was lost, all men, O best of the Bharatas, overpowered by infatuation, became victims of greed. Then they sought to acquire what should not be acquired. Thereby, indeed, O lord, another vice, namely, desire overcame them. Attachment then attacked them, who had become victims of desire. Attached to objects of sense, they did not discriminate between what should be said and what should not be said, between the edible and inedible and between right and wrong. When this world of men had been submerged in dissipation, all spiritual knowledge [brahman] perished; and when spiritual knowledge perished, O king, righteous conduct also perished."

When spiritual knowledge and righteous conduct perished, the gods were overcome with fear, and fearfully sought refuge with Brahma, the creator. Going to the great lord, the ancestor of the worlds, all the gods, afflicted with sorrow, misery, and fear, with folded hands said: "O Lord, the eternal spiritual knowledge, which had existed in the world of men has perished because of greed, infatuation, and the like, therefore we have become fearful. Through the loss of spiritual knowledge, righteous conduct also has perished, O God. Therefore, O Lord of the three worlds, mortals have reached a state of indifference. Verily, we showered rain on earth, but mortals showered rain [i.e., oblations] up to heaven. As a result of the cessation of ritual activity on their part, we faced a serious peril, O grandfather, decide what is most beneficial to use under these circumstances."

Then, the self-born lord said to all those gods: "I will consider what is most beneficial; let your fear depart, O leaders of the gods."

Thereupon he composed a work consisting of a hundred thousand chapters out of his own mind, wherein righteous conduct [dharma], as well as material gain [artha] and enjoyment of sensual pleasures [kama] were described. This group, known as the threefold classification of human objectives, was expounded by the self-born lord; so, too, a fourth objective, spiritual emancipation [moksa], which aims at a different goal, and which constitutes a separate group by itself.

Then the gods approached Vishnu, the lord of creatures, and said: "Indicate to us that one person among mortals who alone is worthy of the highest eminence." Then the blessed lord god Narayana reflected, and brought forth an illustrious mind-born son, called Virajas [who, in this version of the origins of the Indian state, became the first king].(4)

QUESTIONS

1. Historians of world civilization could argue that the passages provided from the <u>Mahabharata</u> describe "a three-stage process in the evolution of government in human society."(5) Select the evidence that supports this statement by briefly quoting each stage you find within the document. Take each quote and paraphrase it. If you are not sure what paraphrase means, use your dictionary to look up the word.

2. Identify all of the characters mentioned in the passage. Select those that you determine to be the main characters. Be prepared to explain your choices.

3. What is the difference between identifying and selecting? How might this difference aid you in interpreting documents; in studying for an examination? Be prepared to discuss these differences in class.

4. Reexamine the entire document recalling what you have learned about selection. Write a brief paragraph that explains the origins of kingship according to the Indian epic <u>Mahabharata</u>.

Endnotes

1. William Duiker and Jackson J. Spielvogel, <u>World History</u> (St. Paul: West Publishing Company, 1993), 50.

2. Walter T. K. Nugent, <u>Creative History: An Introduction to Historical Study</u>, The Lippincott History Series (Philadelphia: J. B. Lippincott Company, 1967), 71, 72.

3. <u>Ibid.</u>, 72-74.

4. Stephen Hay, ed., <u>Sources of Indian Tradition</u> (New York: Columbia University Press), 238-239.

5. Duiker and Spielvogel, <u>World History</u>, 50.

Chapter IV
Change and Continuity in Similar Documents

> On desperate seas long wont to roam,
>   Thy hyacinth hair, thy classic face,
> Thy Naiad airs have brought me home,
>   To the glory that was Greece
>   And the grandeur that was Rome.(1)

"The grandeur that was Rome." Surely you have heard that line from the poem <u>To Helen</u> by Edgar Allan Poe on numerous occasions and in a variety of contexts. Why? What exactly was the grandeur that was Rome? Have you ever thought about it? What would compel a poet, ever so many centuries later, to write such a line? Certainly it must have been something extremely significant. Recall the introduction to this great civilization in your text. If you are unable to do so, return to those pages and reread them. What did you find? Many things obviously, but one is there repeatedly--the ability to govern. This ability, many would agree, was greatly augmented through, not only the establishment of political institutions, but law. Consider the importance of these two factors working together simultaneously. Clearly this combination is of great importance because one alone, as in the case of the Greeks, was a source of weakness. This proved to be especially true when large political entities like empires were established. In short, it might be fair to say that the Greeks were great political theoreticians while the Romans were great political practitioners. As the Oxford University classicist William Warde Fowler (1847-

1921) said of them, "The Romans were, in fact, the most practical people in history; and this enabled them to supply what was wanting to the civilisation of the Mediterranean basin in the work of the Greeks."(2)

An earlier exercise in this volume centered around a law code, the Code of Hammurabi. In light of the foregoing comments on Rome, it seems appropriate at this time to examine another set of laws--the Twelve Tables. The reasoning behind examining more than one law code should be rather self-evident to you. Obviously they are an extremely important historical source and can tell you a great deal about a civilization and its people. Looking at them from a comparative perspective also enables you to reflect on how societies differ; how they are similar; and perhaps, provide some insight into how they evolve over time. Keep this in mind as you read the Twelve Tables with your dictionary at your side.

As for the Tables, best evidence tells us they were compiled somewhere between 451-449 B.C. by a special commission of ten patrician magistrates. Originally inscribed on twelve bronze plaques (thus their name), the Tables were destroyed in 390 B.C. by the invading Gauls. Drawn up in response to pressure exerted by the other class in the early Roman Republic (remember who they were?), the Twelve Tables are of fundamental importance in reconstructing the history of this ancient time period.(3)

DOCUMENT

Selections from the Twelve Tables

Table III: Execution; Law of Debt

When a debt has been acknowledged, or judgment about the matter has been

pronounced in court, thirty days must be the legitimate time of grace. After that, the

debtor may be arrested by laying on of hands. Bring him into court. If he does not satisfy the judgment, or no one in court offers himself as surety in his behalf, the creditor may take the defaulter with him. He may bind him either in stocks or fetters . . . .Unless they make a settlement, debtors shall be held in bond for sixty days. During that time they shall be brought before the praetor's court in the meeting place on three successive market days, and the amount for which they are judged liable shall be announced; on the third market day they shall suffer capital punishment or be delivered up for sale abroad, across the Tiber.

Table IV: Rights of Head of Family

Quickly kill . . . a dreadfully deformed child.

If a father thrice surrender a son for sale, the son shall be free from the father.

A child born ten months after the father's death will not be admitted into a legal inheritance.

Table V: Guardianship; Succession

Females shall remain in guardianship even when they have attained their majority.

If a man is raving mad, rightful authority over his person and chattels shall belong to his agnates or to his classmen.

A spendthrift is forbidden to exercise administration over his own goods . . . . A person who, being insane or a spendthrift, is prohibited from administering his own goods shall be under trusteeship of agnates.

Table VII: Rights Concerning Land

Branches of a tree may be lopped off all round to a height of more than 15 feet . . . . Should a tree on a neighbor's farm be bent crooked by a wind and lean over your farm, action may be taken for removal of that tree.

It is permitted to gather up fruit falling down on another man's farm.

Table VIII: Torts or Delicts

If any person has sung or composed against another person a song such as was causing slander or insult to another, he shall be clubbed to death.

If a person has maimed another's limb, let there be retaliation in kind unless he makes agreement for settlement with him.

Any person who destroys by burning any building or heap of corn deposited alongside a house shall be bound, scourged, and put to death by burning at the stake, provided that he has committed the said misdeed with malice aforethought; but if he shall have committed it by accident that is, by negligence, it is ordained that he repair the damage, or if he be too poor to be competent for such punishment, he shall receive a lighter chastisement.

Table IX: Public Law

The penalty shall be capital punishment for a judge or arbiter legally appointed who has been found guilty of receiving a bribe for giving a decision.

Table XI: Supplementary Laws

Intermarriage shall not take place between plebeians and patricians.(4)

QUESTIONS

After reading the introduction to this chapter and the document under investigation, you should be prepared to answer the questions that follow. Remember to write freely on the document pages as you use the procedures for analysis outlined in Chapter II.

1.   Do you remember the categories the historian uses to organize information? -- political, economic, social, religious, scientific, cultural, and intellectual. Which of these does the Twelve Tables address?

2.   Based on your study of the Roman Republic, are the Tables a good reflection of the society in question? How would you characterize that society using only the evidence in the document?

3.   Based on the evidence provided in the document, would you describe the Twelve Tables as a comprehensive code of laws, that is, one embracing both private and public life? Explain your thoughts in a short paragraph.

4.   Look back at the Code of Hammurabi. Compare and contrast the two documents. Clearly articulate the differences and similarities you find in them. Are these differences and similarities reflective of what you have learned about these two different civilizations? If you had a choice, under which code of laws would you prefer to live?

5.   After examining these two ancient law codes, do you have a better appreciation of your own legal system? Why?

Endnotes

1. <u>The Oxford Dictionary of Quotations</u>, 3rd ed., s.v. "Edgar Allan Poe 1809-1849."

2. W. W. Fowler, <u>Rome</u> (London: Williams and Norgate, 1912), 12, 55-59, 63.

3. M. Cary, <u>A History of Rome Down to the Reign of Constantine</u> (London: Macmillan & Co. LTD, 1965), 41-42.

4. Cicero, <u>Laws</u>, trans. C. W. Keys (Cambridge: Cambridge University Press, 1966) II, xii, 31.

Chapter V
Using Organizational Categories to Answer Historical Questions

Do you recall an earlier chapter in this book where you learned about the groupings or categories historians use to organize their information? Here is another hint to help you: these categories provide insight into fundamental questions involving basic human activities. Correct! The categories in question are political, economic, religious, social, intellectual, scientific, and possibly technological and artistic.

Because these are so critical to the essence of historical study, which is the ability to ask good questions, it is fundamental for you to be able to distinguish them from each other. In many instances this can be rather difficult, especially because the categories may not be mutually exclusive of one another. Consider how true this is as you read and study the following definitions for religious and intellectual history:

> Religious history concerns itself with the persons and forces believed to exist in the supernatural realm. These forces endeavor to explain the otherwise unexplainable. Frequently religious activities, engaged in by the believers, center around an institution like a synagogue, a church, a mosque, or a temple. Believers hold to certain common practices referred to as rituals. Believers also have a shared ethic and faith.

> Intellectual history refers fundamentally to the world of ideas. Usually these ideas are written and expressed in a systematic fashion. Intellectual history

also pertains to the individuals who created the ideas and who systematized them in some way. In a philosophical sense, ideas try to explain how things should be; offer an explanation of why things occur as they do; or explain how certain individuals perceive that things occur.

With these definitions in mind, you will be better prepared to understand why some texts (check your own) consider the life and ideas of the great Chinese thinker, K'ung Fu Tzu, better known as Confucius, to be those of a philosopher rather than those of a religious leader. Two distinguished scholars have therefore written of him that "at first glance the concepts taught seem unexciting and flat to those accustomed to a more rarefied philosophical atmosphere." Furthermore "he does not have the intellectual appeal of a Socrates or a Plato; nor does he fit the pattern of the great religious leaders of India and the Mediterranean world." Most importantly these authors wrote:

> . . . the system that he taught was not a religion in the Western sense. He fully recognized the spirits and Heaven . . . , sometimes showing a sense of mission derived from the latter, but was obviously not much interested in the supra-human realm. . . . He advised respect for the spirits but keeping them at a proper distance. This lack of concern for the other worldly . . . led in time to a strong agnostic strain in the Confucian tradition, which contrasts sharply with the dominant interest in the divine in India and the West.(1)

On the other hand glean the contents of a number of texts concerning themselves with the great religious of the world and you will invariably find Confucius included therein. Why? How is this possible? One such text says of this, "certainly he devoted himself to what he believed were the practical and demanding problems of human beings, society, and government. Yet this was done within the context of a religious frame of reference that included Heaven, Earth, and ancestral spirits . . . ."(2)

With the assistance of your dictionary, examine the excerpt from the <u>Great Learning</u>, which is provided. Answer the questions that follow. They should aid you in determining which organizational category is most appropriate in understanding the work and ideas of Confucius.

DOCUMENT

<u>The Great Learning</u>

The Way of the Great Learning consists in clearly exemplifying illustrious virtue, in loving the people, and in resting in the highest good.

Only when one knows where one is to rest can one have a fixed purpose. Only with a fixed purpose can one achieve calmness of mind. Only with calmness of mind can one attain serene repose. Only in serene repose can one carry on careful deliberation. Only through careful deliberation can one have achievement. Things have their roots and branches; affairs have their beginning and end. He who knows what comes first and what comes last comes himself near the Way.

The ancients who wished clearly to exemplify illustrious virtue throughout the world would first set up good government in their states. Wishing to govern well their states, they would first regulate their families. Wishing to regulate their families, they would first cultivate their persons. Wishing to cultivate their persons, they would first rectify their minds. Wishing to rectify their minds, they would first seek sincerity in their thoughts. Wishing for sincerity in their thoughts, they would first extend their knowledge, the extension of knowledge lay in the investigation of things. For only when things are investigated is knowledge extended; only when knowledge is extended are thoughts sincere; only when thoughts are since are minds rectified; only when our persons are cultivated are our families regulated; only when families are regulated are states well governed; and only when states are well governed is there peace in the world.

From the emperor down to the common people, all, without exception, must consider cultivation of the individual character as the root. If the root is in disorder, it is impossible for the branches to be in order. To treat the important as unimportant and to treat the unimportant as important--this should never be. This is called knowing the root; this is called the perfection of knowledge. . . .(3)

QUESTIONS

1. Based on your understanding of the document and the definitions of religious and intellectual history, categorize the work and the ideas of Confucius. Be prepared to explain your response for a classroom discussion.

2. Reexamine the document and the definitions under investigation. Now try to recategorize the work and the ideas of Confucius. Were you able to do this? Write a concise paragraph of explanation.

3. Could your original categorization have anything to do with your own cultural world view? Think about this as you read the following quote and then pursue a discussion with someone from a different cultural world view:

> The Orientals are an exceedingly concrete, practical, and realistic people; and their religion is best thought of by Westerners as something nearer to what the West regards as aesthetics than it is to what the West has regarded as religion. . . . But in saying this care must be taken. For . . . the aesthetic must be conceived in its Oriental sense as aesthetically immediate for its own sake and not in its Western sense as the handmaiden of commonsense beliefs in external, three-dimensional objects, or of more sophisticated . . . scientific, philosophical, or theological objects. In short, the Oriental uses the purely aesthetic to constitute the nature of the divine. . . .(4)

34

Endnotes

1. Edwin O. Reischauer and John K. Fairbank, <u>A History of East Asian Civilization: East Asia the Great Tradtion, Vol. I</u> (Boston: Houghton Mifflin Company, 1960), 70.

2. Richard C. Bush et al, <u>The Religious World: Communities of Faith</u>, Sec. ed. (New York: Macmillan Publishing Company, 1988), 179.

3. William Theodore De Bary, ed., <u>Sources of Chinese Tradition</u> (New York: Columbia University Press, 1960).

4. F. S. C. Northrop, <u>The Meeting of East and West</u> (New York: The Macmillan Company, 1946), 403-404.

Chapter VI
Careful Examination of Historical Evidence

How much history do you know about the second largest continent in the world? Do you even know which is the second largest in the world? If your answer was Africa, you are correct. Here are some basic facts: Africa covers about one-fifth of the total land surface of the earth--11,700,000 square miles or 30,300,000 square kilometers; Africa has a population of more than 482,000,000 people; Africa is estimated, by various authorities, to have between 800 to more than 1,000 languages; African society was and basically remains one composed of ethnic groups, which number almost 3,000; African religions include not only many of the great religions of the world (Christianity, Islam, Judaism), but also indigenous belief systems; and, Africa contains a very large share of the world's mineral resources. These include, but not inclusively, 25 percent of the world's supply of uranium, almost the entire world's supply of chromium, 68 percent of the world's supply of cobalt, 85 percent of the world's supply of platinum, 54 percent of the world's supply of gold, and the great bulk of the world's supply of diamonds. Furthermore, Africa is most likely the birth continent of humanity.(1)

Considering these facts--were you aware of any of them?--an understanding of the African past is especially important. However these same facts indicate some of the difficulty in studying that past. The size, the diversity, the complexity, the roots of a history over three million years old, have made that task extremely difficult. Examine, very carefully, all of the documents you find in your text that pertain to early Africa. What very interesting difference is there about them, as compared to the documents you have read relating to other civilizations? If you discovered that few, if any of them, were recorded by indigenous peoples, you are definitely on the right track. For despite the deep roots of history on the continent of Africa, a serious, as well as systematic, study of this past coincides only with the "period following the Second World War."(2)

This fact is true, in part, because many African societies did not develop writing. The absence of the written record is especially pronounced in Africa south of the Sahara. It remains so to this day as witnessed by the ! Kung, one of the very last existing traditional gatherer-hunter societies, who call themselves the Zhun/twasi, meaning "the real people." Living in isolated parts of Botswana, Angola, and South West Africa/Namibia, these peoples are speakers of the Khoisan or click languages, specifically North Khoisan (Zhu). As of 1983, "books of ! Kung grammar and vocabulary did not exist, nor did the people themselves read or write."(3)

All of this information raises a host of intriguing dilemmas for historical investigation, especially if you recall what you read in the first chapter of this book about the careful examination of evidence. Perhaps it would be prudent of you to review this information before you examine the three documents below on African history and the questions that follow them. Be sure you have your dictionary as it is almost guaranteed you will need it with these sources!

DOCUMENT 1

The Periplus

Beyond Tabai, after a 400-stade sail along a peninsula towards which, moreover, the

current sets, comes another port of trade, Opone, and it too offers a market for the

aforementioned. Its products for the most part are: cassia; aroma; moto; better-quality slaves, the greater number of which go to Egypt; tortoise shell in great quantity and finer than any other.

Departure from Egypt for all these "far-side" ports of trade is around the month of July, that is Epeiph. To these "far-side" ports of trade it is also common to ship in from the inner regions of Ariake and Barygaza goods from those places that find a market: grain; rice; ghee; sesame oil; cotton cloth, the monache and the sagmatogene [types of cotton cloth from India]; girdles; cane sugar. Some ships sail principally to these ports of trade but some follow the coast and take on whatever cargoes come their way. The area is not ruled by a king but each port of trade is administered by its own chief.

Beyond Opone, with the coast trending more to the south, first come what are called the Small and Great Bluffs of Azania . . . , six runs by now due southwest, then the Small and Great Beaches for another six, and beyond that, in a row, the runs of Azania: first the so-called Sarapion run; then the Nikon; after that numerous rivers and also harbors, one after the other, numbers of them separated by daily stops and runs, seven in all, up to the Pyralaoi Islands and what is called the Canal; from here a little more towards the west, after two night and day runs, lying due west. . . comes Menuthias Island, about 300 stades from the mainland. It is low and wooded and has rivers, a wide variety of birds, and mountain tortoise. There are no wild animals at all except crocodiles; these, however, are not harmful to humans. The island has sewn boats and dugout canoes that are used for fishing and for catching turtles. The inhabitants of this island also have their own way of going after these with baskets, which they lower instead of nets around the mouths of [rocky inlets].

Two runs beyond this island comes the very last port of trade on the coast of Azania, called Rhapta ["sewn"], a name derived from the aforementioned sewn boats, where there are great quantities of ivory and tortoise shell. Very big-bodied men, tillers of the soil, inhabit the region; these behave, each in his own place, just like chiefs. The region is under the rule of the governor of Mapharitis, since by some ancient right it is subject to the kingdom of Arabia as first constituted. The mechants of Muza hold it through a grant from the king and collect taxes from it. They send out to it merchant craft that they staff mostly with Arab skippers and agents who, through continual intercourse and intermarriage, are familiar with the area and its language.

The principal imports into these ports of trade are: spears from Muza of local workmanship; axes; knives; small awls; numerous types of glass stones. Also, to certain places, wine and grain in considerable quantity, not for trade but as an expenditure of the good will of the Barbaroi. The area exports: a great amount of ivory but inferior to that from Adulis; rhinoceros horn; best-quality tortoise shell after the Indian; a little nautilus shell.

These are just about the very last ports of trade on the coast of Azania to the right of Berenice. For, beyond this area lies unexplored ocean that bends to the west and, extending on the south along the parts of Ethiopia and Libya and Africa that turn away, joins the western sea.(4)

DOCUMENT 2

Al Bakri's Description of Ghana

The king's residence comprises a palace and conical huts, the whole surrounded by a fence like a wall. Around the royal town are huts and groves of thorn trees where live the magicians who control their religious rites. These groves, where they keep their idols and bury their kings, are protected by guards who permit no one to enter or find out what goes on in them.

None of those who belong to the imperial religion may wear tailored garments except the king himself and the heir-presumptive, his sister's son. The rest of the people wear wrappers of cotton, silk or brocade according to their means. Most of the men shave their beards and the women their heads. The king adorns himself with female ornaments around the neck and arms. On his head he wears gold-embroidered caps covered with turbans of finest cotton. He gives audience to the people for the redressing of grievances in a hut around which are placed 10 horses covered in golden cloth. Behind him stand 10 slaves carrying shields and swords mounted with gold. On his right are the sons of vassal kings, their heads plaited with gold and wearing costly garments. On the ground around him are seated his ministers, whilst the governor of the city sits before him. On guard at the door are dogs of fine pedigree, wearing collars adorned with gold and silver. The royal audience is announced by the beating of a drum, called daba, made out of a long piece of hollowed-out wood. When the people have gathered, his co-religionists draw near upon their knees sprinkling dust upon their heads as a sign of respect, whilst the Muslims clap hands as their form of greeting.(5)

DOCUMENT 3

Leo Africanus, The History and Description of Africa

The large province of Borno bordering westward upon the province of Guangana, and from thence extending eastward five hundred miles, is distant from the fountain of Niger almost one hundred and fifty miles, the south part thereof adjoining unto the desert of Set, and the north part unto that desert which lieth towards Barca. The situation of this kingdom is very uneven, some part thereof being mountainous, and the residue plain. Upon the plains are sundry villages inhabited by rich merchants, and abounding with corn. The king of this region and all his followers dwell in a certain large village. The mountains inhabited by herdsmen and shepherds do bring forth millet and other grain altogether unknown to us. The inhabitants in summer go all naked save their private members which they cover with a piece of leather: but all winter they are clad in skins, and have beds of skins also. They embrace no religion at all, being neither Christians, Mahumetans, nor Jews, nor of any other profession, but living after a brutish manner, and having wives and children in common: and (as I understand among them) they have no proper names at all, but every one is nicknamed according to his length, his fatness, or some other quality. They have a most puissant prince, being lineally descended from the Libyan people called Bardoa. Horsemen he hath in a continual readiness to the number of three thousand, and a huge number of footmen; for all his subjects are so serviceable and obedient unto him, that whensoever he commandeth them, they will arm themselves and follow him whither he pleaseth to conduct them. They pay unto him none other tribute but the tithes of all their corn; neither hath this king any revenues to maintain his estate, but only such spoils as he getteth from his next enemies by often invasions and assaults. He is at perpetual enmity with a certain people inhabiting beyond the desert of Sau; who in times past marching with a huge army of footmen over the said desert, wasted a great part of the kingdom of Borno. Whereupon the king of Borno sent for the merchants of Barbary, and willed them to bring him great

store of horses; for in this country they use to exchange horses for slaves, and to

give fifteen, and sometimes twenty slaves for one horse.(6)

QUESTIONS

1. Characterize the focus of each of the three documents. How much does each author focus on the natural features of the environment versus the human inhabitants and their culture? Why might one be emphasized more than the other? Explain your thoughts briefly in preparation for the rest of the questions that follow.

2. Do you detect bias on the part of any of the authors? Identify the nature of that bias--cultural, religious--for example. In each case that you find bias, explain in a brief paragraph why this is important to determine. For example, in what ways might future readers be misled by the document?

3. Considering the importance of the written word to the Western mind, how might its absence have influenced the thinking about the African past? Be prepared to discuss your answer with another member of your history class.

4. Having read this chapter and the documents, write a two hundred word essay on the importance of carefully examining documentary evidence, especially when it is cross-cultural.

44

Endnotes

1. <u>Encyclopaedia Britannica</u>, 15 ed., s.v. "Africa;" "African Languages;" and, "African Peoples and Cultures."

2. J. F. Ade Ajayi and Ian Espie, eds., <u>A Thousand Years of West African History</u> (Ibadan, Nigeria: Ibadan University Press and Nelson, 1965), 1.

3. Marjorie Shostak, <u>Nisa: The Life and Words of a ! Kung Woman</u> (New York: Random House, 1981; Vintage Book, 1983), 4; 17.

4. <u>The Periplus Maris Erythraei</u>, ed. Lionel Casson (Princeton: Princeton University Press, 1989), 59-61.

5. J. S. Trimingham, <u>A History of Islam and West Africa</u> (New York: Oxford University Press, 1970), 55.

6. Leo Africanus, <u>The History and Description of Africa</u> (New York: Burt Franklin), 833.

Chapter VII
Historical Generalization

In the two preceding chapters you have been grappling with issues centering on interpretation as a part of the historical process. Another extremely important component in this process is that of making generalizations. Can you define this term as it applies to history? Now read the following: "Theoretically, a historical generalization is a statement or term which has been inferred inductively from a number of particular cases, instances, or events."(1)

This definition of generalization should have taken you full circle intellectually-- right back to our beginning chapter where it was discovered that the definition of history meant a process of inquiry. To put this concisely, "the historical generalization suggests some regularity or pattern of events, ideas, and human actions which is of historical significance."(2)

Stop here and test your ability to recall and apply what you have learned from these exercises and the information in your text. What very famous ancient historian was attempting to use a historical generalization when he wrote "it will be enough for me . . . if these words of mine are judged useful by those who want to understand clearly the events which happened in the past and which (human nature being what it is) will at some time or other and in much the same ways, be repeated in the future. My work is not a piece of writing designed to meet the taste of an immediate public, but was done to last for ever."(3) Identify the generalization that has been made by rephrasing it in your own words. Most historians agree that generalizations vary in gradations of inclusiveness. The simplest forms are one word labels--Jews, Christians, Muslims.(4) A more complex form of generalization serves to connect and interpret information. Obviously this level of use is extremely important for historical investigation. Not only does it put concepts and facts into meaningful relationship, it also helps to establish why and how certain events took place.(5)

Other forms of generalization operate at higher levels, but historians are not so prone to use them because they are quite unreliable. Our quote from Thucydides would be an example of a generalization of the highest degree of inclusiveness. Is he not seeking to find underlying principles of human behavior? Reread the quote.

Now examine the documents that follow. Each one is taken from three of the great religions in the world that you should have studied by this time in your course work. Follow the procedures you have used in the past as you work your way through the materials.

DOCUMENT 1

Psalm 8

O Lord, our Lord,

how majestic is thy name in all the earth!

Thou whose glory above the heavens is

> chanted

> by the mouth of babes and infants,

thou hast founded a bulwark because of thy

foes,

to still the enemy and the avenger.

When I look at thy heavens, the work of thy

fingers,

the moon and the stars which thou hast

established;

what is man that thou art mindful of him,

and the son of man that thou dost care for

him?

Yet thou hast made him little less than God,

and dost crown him with glory and honor.

Thou hast given him dominion over the works

of thy hands;

thou hast put all things under his feet,

all sheep and oxen,

and also the beasts of the field,

the birds of the air, and the fish of the sea,

whatever passes along the paths of the sea.

O Lord, our Lord

how majestic is thy name in all the earth!(6)

DOCUMENT 2

<u>The Gospel According to St. John</u>

In the beginning was the Word, and the Word was with God, and the Word was God. The same was in the beginning with God. All things were made by him; and without him was not any thing made that was made. In him was life; and the light of men. And the light shineth in darkness; and the darkness comprehended it not.

There was a man sent from God, whose name was John. The same came from a witness, to bear witness of the Light that all men through him might believe. He was not that Light, but was sent to bear witness of the Light, that all men through him might believe. That was the true Light, which lighteth every man that cometh into the world. He was in the world, and the world was made by him, and world knew not him. He came unto his own, and his own received him not. But as many as recived him, to them gave he power to become the sons of God, even to them that believe on his name: which were born, not of blood, nor of the will of the flesh, nor

of the will of man, but of God. And the Word was made flesh, and dwelt among us

(and we beheld his glory, the glory as of the only begotten of the Father), full of

grace and truth.(7)

DOCUMENT 3

The Koran

Say: HE IS ONE GOD:

God the Eternal.

He begetteth not, nor is begotten;

Nor is there one like unto Him.

Magnify the name of thy LORD, THE MOST HIGH,

Who created, and fashioned,

And decreed, and guided

Who bringeth forth the pasturage,

Then turneth it dry and brown.

We will make thee cry aloud, and thou shall not forget,

Except what God pleaseth; verily He knoweth the plain and hidden.

And will speed thee to ease.

Admonish, therefore--verily admonishing profiteth,--

Whoso feareth God will mind;

And there will turn away from it only the wretch

Who shall broil upon the mighty fire,

And then shall neither die therein, nor live.

Happy is he who purifieth himself,

And remembereth the name of his Lord, and prayeth.(8)

QUESTIONS

1. How many generalizations are you able to make about the documents?

2. Make different levels of generalizations from these documents. Is this more difficult to do? Think about the reasons and explain them in a paragraph or two.

3. With the three documents in mind, read the quote provided below and identify the type of generalization it makes.

    > Most men . . . do not think that men are all that matters.
    > To think this is to run counter to a very deep feeling,
    > namely, that man de-pends for life and fullness of being
    > on forces outside himself that share in some sense his own
    > nature and with which he must be in harmony. The
    > harmony thus sought is sometimes a harmony in action . . .
    > or it is a moral and spiritual harmony . . . or the harmony
    > sought is more than a harmony, it is a complete and final
    > identity . . . .(9)

4. Based on your reading of the documents, would you maintain that the above quote is an accurate generalization? Explain why or why not.

Endnotes

1. Lester D. Stephens, <u>Probing the Past: A Guide to the Study and Teaching of History</u> (Boston: Allyn and Bacon, Inc., 1974), 66.

2. <u>Ibid</u>.

3. Thucydides, <u>History of the Peloponnesian Wars</u>, trans. Rex Warner (Harmondsworth, England: Penguin Books, 1972), 324.

4. Walter T. K. Nugent, <u>Creative History: An Introduction to Historical Study</u>, The Lippincott History Series (Philadelphia: J. B. Lippincott Company, 1967), 76.

5. Stephens, <u>Probing the Past</u>, 68.

6. Revised Standard Version of the Bible (Division of Christian Education of the National Council of the Churches of Christ in the USA, 1971).

7. George H. Knoles and Rixford K. Snyder, eds., <u>Readings in Western Civilization</u>, 3rd ed. (Chicago: J. B. Lippincott Company, 1960), 170.

8. Stanley Lane-Poole, <u>The Speech-and-Table-Talk of the Prophet Mohammed</u> (London: Macmillan, 1905), 15, 32, 83, 133-137.

9. John B. Noss, <u>Man's Religions</u>, 3rd ed. (New York: The Macmillan Company, 1963), 3.

Chapter VIII
Comparative History

Echoing Simone De Beauvoir's seminal work, <u>The Second Sex</u>, two contemporary social scientists, Carol Travis and Carole Offir wrote, "men and women have never shared power, privilege, and status on an equal basis."(1)   Quite a sweeping statement isn't it? Historically speaking, how would you label it--a generalization; a law?   Your task will be to determine its accuracy across various non-Western cultures.

In undertaking this task as your objective, "the systematic comparison of some process or institution in two or more societies that are not usually cojoined within one of the traditionally geographical areas of historical specialization,"(2) you are going to engage in comparative history. Of course in order to do this well one must be knowledgeable in the history of all the societies he or she compares. This is not an easy task. Think about it. Being knowledgeable about the history of any single country is difficult enough. You should certainly be appreciating this fact more and more as you progress through your own introduction to World Civilization.

What follows, then, are five documents dealing with women in their respective societies including: India; China; Africa; Japan; and Vietnam. A variety of pitfalls await you as you attempt to do your comparisons. To prepare yourself, refer back to your text and refamiliarize yourself with the history of each area.   Read the documents in question very carefully.   Pay special note to their gender, their religious beliefs, their national origin. All of the documents are followed by a series of questions for you to consider.

DOCUMENT 1

Excerpt from <u>Sources of Indian Tradition</u>

Women must be honored and adorned by their father, brothers, husbands, and brother-in-law who desire great good fortune.

Where women, verily, are honored, there the gods rejoice; where, however, they are not honored, there all sacred rites prove fruitless.

Where the female relations live in grief--that family soon perishes completely; where, however, they do not suffer from any grievance--that family always prospers.

. . .

Her father protects her in childhood, her husband protects her in youth, her sons protect her in old age--a woman does not deserve independence.

The father who does not give away his daughter in marriage at the proper time is censurable; censurable is the husband who does not approach his wife in due season; and after the husband is dead, the son, verily is censurable, who does not protect his mother.

Even against the slightest provocations should women be particularly guarded; for unguarded they would bring grief to both the families.

Regarding this as the highest dharma of all four classes, husbands, though weak, must strive to protect their wives.

His own offspring, character, family, self, and dharma does one protect when he protects his wife scrupulously. . . .

The husband should engage his wife in the collection and expenditure of his wealth, in cleanliness, in dharma, in cooking food for the family, and in looking after the necessities of the household. . . .

Women destined to bear children, enjoying great good fortune, deserving of worship, the resplendent lights of homes on the one hand and divinities of good luck who reside in the houses on the other--between these there is no difference whatsoever.(3)

DOCUMENT 2

<u>Ban Zhao, prominent female historian of the Han Dynasty on the Role of Women</u>

To be humble, yielding, respectful and reverential; to put herself after others . . . these qualities are those exemplifying woman's low and humble estate. To retire late and rise early; not to shirk exertion from dawn to dark . . . this is called being diligent. To behave properly and decorously in serving her husband; to be serene and self-possessed, shunning jest and laughter . . . this is called being worthy of continuing the husband's lineage. If a woman possess the above mentioned three qualities, then her reputation shall be excellent.(4)

DOCUMENT 3

Leo Africanus, <u>The History and Description of Africa</u>

Their women (according to the guise of that country) go very gorgeously attired: they wear linen gowns dyed black, with exceeding wide sleeves, over which sometimes they cast a mantle of the same colour or of blue, the corners of which mantle are very artificially fastened about their shoulders with a fine silver clasp. Likewise they have rings hanging at their ears, which for the most part are made of silver; they wear many rings also upon their fingers. Moreover they usually wear about their thighs and ankles certain scarfs and rings, after the fashion of the Africans. They cover their faces with certain masks having only two holes for the eyes to peep out at. If any man chance to meet with them, they presently hide their faces, passing by him with silence, except it be some of their allies or kinsfolks; for unto them they always discover their faces, neither is there any use of the said mask so long as they be in presence. These Arabians when they travel any journey (as they oftentimes do) they set their women upon certain saddles made handsomely of wicker for the same purpose, and fastened to their camel backs, neither be they anything too wide, but fit only for a woman to sit in. When they go to the wars each man carries his wife with him, to the end that she may cheer up her good man, and give him encouragement. Their damsels which are unmarried do usually paint their faces, breasts, arms, hands, and fingers with a kind of counterfeit colour: which is accounted a most decent custom among them.(5)

DOCUMENT 4

<u>A Buddhist's Commentary, "On the Salvation of Women"</u>

We must admit that there are great hindrances in the way of woman's attaining enlightenment . . . the reason is that her sin is grievous, and so she is not allowed to enter the lofty palace of the great Brahma, nor to look upon the clouds which hover over his ministers and people. She is always taken down to a lower seat than the soft-cushioned one of the divine, Indra, and she can never behold the flowers in his thirty-three-citied Heaven. . . .(6)

DOCUMENT 5

<u>18th Century Vietnamese Historian</u>

The imperial court was far away; local officials were greedy and oppressive. At that time the county of one hundred sons was the county of the women of Lord To. The ladies [the Trung Sisters] used the female arts against their irreconcilable foe; skirts and hairpins sang of patriotic righteousness, uttered a solemn oath at the inner door of the ladies quarters, expelled the governor, and seized the capital. . . . Were they not grand heroines? . . . Our two ladies brought forward an army of all the people, and, establishing a royal court that settled affairs in the territories of the sixty-five strongholds, shook their skirts over the Hundred Yueh [the Vietnamese people].(7)

QUESTIONS

1. List any common themes you find regarding the treatment of women in the five documents.

2. Identify any differences you find regarding the view of women in the five documents.

3. Identify the documents where religion enters into the proper role ascribed to the women of the society. Characterize that role. What are the religions and research their attitudes about women. Briefly note what you find for future reference.

4. Reexamine Document 1 and Document 2. Would you be surprised, based on what Document 1 says, that Indian society practiced sati? Condemned only in the last century, sati is currently experiencing something of a revival in contemporary India. The practice involves widowed women immolating themselves on their husband's funeral pyres.(8) Write a paragraph explaining your response to this practice. Would you be surprised, based on your understanding of Document 2, that Chinese women bound their feet with little governmental opposition until it was criticized by the Nationalists around 1911. When the Communist Chinese came into power in 1949, the practice was outlawed officially. If you don't know anything about footbinding, go do some digging in a library and read about it.

5. Write an essay, around two hundred words, addressing the quote given at the beginning of this chapter--"men and women have never shared power, privilege, and status on an equal basis."

60

Endnotes

1. Carol Travis and Carole Offir, <u>The Longest War: Sex Differences in Perspective</u> (New York: Harcourt Brace Jovanovich, Inc., 1977), 3.

2. George M. Fredrickson, "Comparative History," in <u>The Past Before Us: Contemporary Historical Writing in the United States</u>, ed. Michael Kammen (Ithaca, N.Y.: Cornell University Press, 1980), 458.

3. Stephen Hay, ed., <u>Sources of Indian Tradition</u> (New York: Columbia University Press, 1988).

4. R. H. van Gulick, <u>Sexual Life in Ancient China</u> (Leiden: Brill, 1961), 98-99.

5. Leo Africanus, <u>The History and Description of Africa</u> (New York: Burt Franklin), 158-159.

6. David John Lu, ed., Japan: <u>A Documentary History</u>, (Armonk, New York: M. E. Sharpe, 1997), 131-132.

7. Keith W. Taylor, <u>The Birth of Vietnam</u> (Berkeley, California: The University of California, 1983), 336-37.

8. A. L. Basham, <u>The Wonder that Was India: A Survey of the Culture of the Indian Sub-Continent Before the Coming of the Muslims</u> (New York: Grove Press, Inc., 1959), 187.

Chapter IX
Digging for Evidence

Make a list of sources you think some student a millenium from now would consult if he or she wished to discover the kinds of foods that were consumed in 20th century American society. Examine your list and see how many of those sources might have been available a millenium earlier. Not too many, right? Given you find this to be true, what source materials would you use to answer this important question about that period in time known generally as the Middle Ages? Below is a very brief list of possibilities:

1. Records from monasteries
2. Personal records and correspondence
3. Official records of knight's households
4. Guild records
5. Information about holiday and ceremonial feasts
6. Cooking manuals/cookbooks
7. Works of art
8. Poetry

Some of these possibilities should be of no surprise to you based on what you have already learned about this period in history. But what of the last three? Do you find it interesting to discover that cooking manuals or cookbooks existed? Did you assume they have always existed? One famous cooking manual, compiled by the master cooks of England's Richard II around 1390, was entitled <u>The Forme of Cury</u>. Here, for example, is a recipe for "salat": "Take parsel, sawge, garlec, chibollas . . ., oynons, leek, borage, myntes, porrectes . . . , fenel, and ton tressis . . . , rew, rosemarye, purslarye . . . ; lave, and woisshe hem clene; pike hem, pluk hem small with thyn . . . honde, and myng . . . hem ind raw oile. Lay on vynegar and salt, and serve it forth."(1)

A slightly older cookbook from France, a culture very often associated with excellent food, is that by Guillaume Tirel. Beginning as a mere scullion, he went on to work in the service of Philip VI of Valois and the Dauphin; was called to the kitchens of Charles V; and then, in 1375 wrote <u>Le Viandier</u>, the oldest French cookbook known to exist. Famous in its own day, it has remained so up to the present. In fact, <u>Le Viandier</u> is one of the first books to be put in print. Taillevent, as he liked to call himself, was much concerned with the secrets of making fine sauces, sops, and vegtables. Sops were an early form of pureed soups. They were made of wine flavored milk, saffron, and honey or other sweetners. Dead at the age of sixty-nine, Taillevent was buried beneath a tombstone picturing him in the dress of a sergeant at arms. Appropriately, his shield was embellished with three cooking pots.(2)

Early or late in their appearance, cookbooks are a most obvious source of information about dietary preferences. Did you ever think the final two on the list of possibilities could yield this type of information? Go to your own textbook and several others to look for illustrations of medieval art. What did you find? If little, dig further. Visit your college or university library and seek out art histories of the period. Note the things you find and put them aside for now.

Poetry! Probably you never ever considered this as a source. Yet one of the greatest masterpieces of world literature, Chaucer's <u>Canterbury Tales</u>, says much about food. Examine the excerpts provided. Answer the questions that follow as you interpret Chaucer.

DOCUMENT

> There also was a <u>Nun</u>, a Prioress,
>
> Her way of smiling very simple and coy.
>
> Her greatest oath was only 'By St Loy!'
>
> And she was known as Madam Eglantyne.
>
> And well she sang a service, with a fine
>
> Intoning through her nose, as was most seemly,
>
> And she spoke daintily in French, extremely,
>
> After the school of Stratford-atte-Bowe;
>
> French in the Paris style she did not know.
>
> At meat her manners were well taught withal;
>
> No morsel from her lips did she let fall,
>
> Nor dipped her fingers in the sauce too deep;
>
> But she could carry a morsel up and keep
>
> The smallest drop from falling on her breast.
>
> For courtliness she had a special zest,
>
> And she would wipe her upper lip so clean

That not a trace of grease was to be seen

Upon the cup when she had drunk; to eat,

She reached a hand sedately for the meat.

She certainly was very entertaining,

Pleasant and friendly in her ways, and straining

To counterfeit a courtly kind of grace,

A stately bearing fitting to her place,

And to seem dignified in all her dealings.

As for her sympathies and tender feelings,

She was so charitably solicitous

She used to weep if she but saw a mouse

Caught in a trap, if it were dead or bleeding.

And she had little dogs she would be feeding

With roasted flesh, or milk, or fine white bread.

And bitterly she wept if one were dead

Or someone took a stick and made it smart;
She was all sentiment and tender heart. . . .

. . . .

A <u>Monk</u> there was, one of the finest sort

Who rode the country; hunting was his sport.

A manly man, to be an Abbot able;

Many a dainty horse he had in stable.

His bridle, when he rode, a man might hear

Jingling in a whistling wind as clear,

Aye, and as loud as does the chapel bell

Where my lord Monk was Prior of the cell.

The Rule of good St Benet or St Maur

As old and strict he tended to ignore;

He let go by the things of yesterday

And took the modern world's more spacious way.

He did not rate that text at a plucked hen

Which says that hunters are not holy men

And that a monk uncloistered is a mere

Fish out of water, flapping on the pier,

That is to say a monk out of his cloister.

That was a text he held not worth an oyster;

And I agreed and said his views were sound;

Was he to study till his head went round

Poring over books in cloisters? Must he toil

As Austin bade and till the very soil?

Was he to leave the world upon the shelf?

Let Austin have his labour to himself.

      . . . .

This Monk was therefore a good man to horse;

Greyhounds he had, as swift as birds, to course.

Hunting a hare or riding at a fence

Was all his fun, he spared for no expense.

I saw his sleeves were garnished at the hand

With fine grey fur, the finest in the land,

And on his hood, to fasten it at his chin

He had a wrought-gold cunningly fashioned pin;

Into a lover's knot it seemed to pass.

His head was bald and shone like looking-glass;

So did his face, as if it had been greased.

He was a fat and personable priest;

His prominent eyeballs never seemed to settle.

They glittered like the flames beneath a kettle;

Supple his boots, his horse in fine condition.

He was a prelate fit for exhibition,

He was not pale like a tormented soul.

He liked a fat swan best, and roasted whole.

His palfrey was as brown as is a berry.

.   .   .   .

There was a <u>Franklin</u> with him, it appeared;

White as a daisy-petal was his beard.

A sanguine man, high-coloured and benign,

He loved a morning sop of cake in wine.

He lived for pleasure and had always done,

For he was Epicurus' very son,

In whose opinion sensual delight

Was the one true felicity in sight.

As noted as St Julian was for bounty

He made his household free to all the County.

His bread, his ale were finest of the fine

And no one had a better stock of wine.

His house was never short of bake-meat pies,

Of fish and flesh, and these in such supplies

It positively snowed with meat and drink

And all the dainties that a man could think.

According to the seasons of the year

Changes of dish were ordered to appear.

He kept fat partridges in coops, beyond,

Many a bream and pike were in his pond.

Woe to the cook unless the sauce was hot

And sharp, or if he wasn't on the spot!

And in his hall a table stood arrayed

And ready all day long, with places laid. . . .(3)

QUESTIONS

1. What kinds of foods are mentioned in the <u>Tales</u>? Is there a considerable variety of food discussed in the poem? How many? List them.

2. Does it appear that food and drink are abundant? Does it seem that food and drink are important?

3. Find any descriptions of table manners. Describe them. Of what significance is this? How does it compare were someone to read this alongside Miss Manners or Emily Post?

4. Go back to the list of things you found when looking through your text and art books on the Middle Ages. How do these compare with what was in the <u>Canterbury Tales</u>? Write a brief essay on food and its importance in the Middle Ages.

5. If this topic is of particular interest to you, go further. Examine other works of poetry like <u>Carmina Burana</u>, and William Langland's <u>Piers the Ploughman</u>. Bon appetit!

Endnotes

1. William Harlan Hale and the editors of <u>Horizon Magazine</u>, <u>The Horizon Cookbook and Illustrated History of Eating and Drinking through the Ages</u> (Garden City, New York: American Heritage Publishing Co., Inc., 1968), 87.

2. <u>Ibid</u>., 85.

3. Geoffrey Chaucer, <u>The Canterbury Tales</u>, trans. Nevill Coghill (London: Penguin Books, 1951), 22-25; 28-29.

Chapter X
Philosophies of History

Surely you have heard the expression "History repeats itself." Exactly what is the nature of such an expression? Is it merely another example of an historical generalization like those you learned to identify in Chapter VII? In a way yes it is, but it is more. It is more because it comes close to resembling a "law." A law because "it implies unvarying regularity" and therefore it might well be labeled a "predictive generalization."(1)

However true this might be, a predictive generalization is more and therefore better identified as a philosophy of history. "A philosophy of history is a systematizing of human knowledge and thought within the realm of historical fact." Furthermore, it is solely the personal judgment and interpretation of its originator and like believers who ascribe to it.(2)

Does this mean it is of no value to students of history like you? Quite to the contrary. Ponder the definition and the key words anew--systematizing; human knowledge and thought; and realm of historical fact. Is this not thought provoking? Does it not reaffirm the essential rationale for studying history as previously discussed? Could it not exert an influence on world events? Think of a philosophy of history that has exerted just such an influence.

At least three distinct philosophies of history can be identified. They include the cyclical (possibly fatalistic), the providential, and the progressive. By cyclical we really are saying that history repeats itself--history runs in cycles. In the Western world such a view prevailed from the time of the father of history, Herodotus, to the advent of Christianity. It could be argued it remains the paramount philosophy of history in many parts of the world today--China, for example. The providential view of history emerged in the early Christian Era and maintained that the decisive event in history was the life of Christ "before which all mankind had been doomed, and after which all of the elect were saved."(3) The progressive philosophy of history fully developed around the early 18th century. Simply put, "mankind is getting better and better."(4) Do the providential and progressive philosophies sound the same to you? Examine the definitions again to determine how they differ.

Given these philosophies of history, how might you, the student, account for the rise and fall of great civilizations? Examine the two documents provided you that deal with the Muslim empires. Address yourself to the questions that come after them.

DOCUMENT 1

So saying, he [the Sultan] led them himself. And they, with a shout on the run and with a fearsome yell, went on ahead of the Sultan, pressing on up to the palisade. After a long and bitter struggle they hurled back the Romans [Byzantines] from there and climbed by force up the palisade. They dashed some of their foe down into the ditch between the great wall and the palisade, which was deep and hard to get out of, and they killed them there. The rest they drove back to the gate.

He had opened this gate in the great wall, so as to go easily over to the palisade. Now there was a great struggle there and great slaughter among those stationed there, for they were attacked by the heavy infantry and not a few others in irregular formation, who had been attracted from many points by the shouting. There the Emperor Constantine [Constantine XIII Palaeologus], with all who were with him, fell in gallant combat.

The heavy infantry were already streaming through the little gate into the City, and others had rushed in through the breach in the great wall. Then all the rest of the army, with a rush and a roar, poured in brilliantly and scattered all over the City. And the Sultan stood before the great wall, where the standard also was and the ensigns, and watched the proceedings. The day was already breaking. . . .

The soldiers fell on them [the citizens] with anger and great wrath. For one thing, they were actuated by the hardships of the siege. For another, some foolish people had hurled taunts and curses at them from the battlements all through the siege. Now, in general they killed so as to frighten all the City, and to terrorize and enslave all by the slaughter.

When they had had enough of murder, and the City was reduced to slavery, some of the troops turned to the mansions of the mighty, by bands and companies and divisions, for plunder and spoil. Others went to the robbing of churches, and others dispersed to the simple homes of the common people, stealing, robbing, plundering, killing, insulting, taking and enslaving men, women, and children, old and young, priests, monks--in short, every age and class. . . .

They say that many of the maidens, even at the mere unaccustomed sight and sound of these men, were terror-stricken and came near losing their very lives. And there were also honorable old men who were dragged by their white hair, and some of them beaten unmercifully. And well-born and beautiful young boys were carried off. . . .

After this the Sultan entered the City and looked about to see its great size, its situation, its grandeur and beauty, its teeming population, its loveliness, and the costliness of its churches and public buildings and of the private houses and community houses and those of the officials. . . . When he saw what a large number had been killed, and the ruin of the buildings, and the wholesale ruin and destruction of the City, he was filled with compassion and repented not a little at the destruction and plundering. Tears fell from his eyes as he groaned deeply and passionately: "What a city we have given over to plunder and destruction."

Thus he suffered in spirit. And indeed this was a great blow to us, in this one city, a disaster the like of which had occurred in no one of the great renowned cities of history, whether one speaks of the size of the captured City or of the bitterness and harshness of the deed. And no less did it astound all others than it did those who went through it and suffered, through the unreasonable and unusual character of the event and through the over-whelming and unheard-of horror of it.

As for the great City of Constantine, raised to a great height of glory and dominion and wealth in its own times, overshadowing to an infinite degree all the cities around it, renowned for its glory, wealth, authority, power, and greatness, and all its other qualities, it thus came to its end.(5)

DOCUMENT 2

They made one or two very poor charges on our right and left divisions. My troops making use of their bows, plied them with arrows, and drove them in upon their center. The troops on the right and the left of their center, being huddled together in one place, such confusion ensued, that the enemy, while totally unable to advance, found also no road by which they could flee. The sun had mounted spear-high when the onset of battle began, and the combat lasted till midday, when the enemy were completely broken and routed, and my friends victorious and exulting. By the grace and mercy of Almighty God, this arduous undertaking was rendered easy for me, and this mighty army, in the space of half a day, laid in the dust. Five or six thousand men were discovered lying slain, in one spot, near Ibrahim. We reckoned that the number lying slain, in different parts of this field of battle, amounted to fifteen or sixteen thousand men. On reaching Agra, we found, from the accounts of the natives of Hindustan, that forty or fifty thousand men had fallen in this field. After routing the enemy, we continued the pursuit, slaughtering, and making them prisoners. Those who were ahead, began to bring in the Amirs and Afghans as prisoners. They brought in a very great number of elephants with their drivers, and offered them to me as peshkesh. Having pursued the enemy to some distance, and supposing that Ibrahim had escaped from the battle, I appointed Kismai Mirza, Baba Chihreh, and Bujkeh, with a party of my immediate adherents, to follow him in close pursuit down as far as Afra. Having passed through the middle of Ibrahim's camp, and visited his pavilions and accommodations, we encamped on the banks of the Siah-ab.

It was now afternoon prayers when Tahir Taberi, the younger brother of Khalifeh, having found Ibrahim lying dead amidst a number of slain, cut off his head, and brought it in. . . .

Yet, under such circumstances, and in spite of this power, placing my trust in God, and leaving behind me my old and inveterate enemy the Uzbeks, who had an army of a hundred thousand men, I advanced to meet so powerful a prince as Sultan Ibrahim, the lord of numerous armies, and emperor of extensive territories. In consideration of my confidence in Divine aid, the Most High God did not suffer the distress and hardships that I had undergone to be thrown away, but defeated my formidable enemy, and made me the conqueror of the noble country of Hindustan. This success I do not ascribe to my own strength, nor did this good fortune flow from my own efforts, but from the fountain of the favor and mercy of God.(6)

QUESTIONS

1. You are the philosopher of history and therefore free to make a personal judgment and interpretation. Ascribe a philosophy of history to each of the two documents in question. Explain your choice(s). Be prepared to defend them in a classroom discussion.

2. Given what you have learned about Islam and the various Muslim civilizations, what philosophy of history do you think is most applicable to them? Why? Explain carefully in a short paragraph.

3. Make an appointment with a philosophy or religion professor who is especially knowledgeable on this part of the world to find out if you answered the question above correctly. If you were not correct, reexamine the philosophies of history discussed in this chapter.

Endnotes

1. Lester D. Stephens, <u>Probing the Past: A Guide to the Study and Teaching of History</u> (Boston: Allyn and Bacon, Inc., 1974), 70.

2. Donald V. Gawronski, <u>History: Meaning and Method</u> (Iowa City: Sernoll, Inc., 1967), 19.

3. Allan Nevins, <u>The Gateway to History</u>, Rev. ed. (Boston: D. C. Heath and Company, 1938; Garden City, New York: Doubleday & Company, Inc., Anchor Books, 1962), 265.

4. Gawronski, <u>History</u>, 22.

5. William H. McNeill and M. R. Waldham, <u>The Islamic World</u> (Chicago: The University of Chicago Press, 1973), 331-335.

6. <u>The Memoirs of Zehir-ed-Din Muhammed</u> Baber, trans. John Leyden and William Erskine (London: Longman and Cadell, 1826).

Chapter XI
Understanding Cultural Transformation

Surely at this point in your course of study, a better realization of the complexity of your task has become apparent. You are in fact trying to come to some understanding of humanity and its historical variations throughout time and place. Indeed an ambitious objective! One possible way to help achieve this objective is by examining the ways in which different peoples and different cultures reacted, interacted, and were transformed by each other. Be sure you note the words transformed by each other, for all groups do change, however imperceptibly it may seem, as a consequence of their contact. Too often this is not understood even by very sophisticated minds; especially when those minds have been trained in one world, the Occidental for example. Thus attempts are made to impose "Western-inspired schemes . . . to East Asia. . . ." whether they fit very well or not.(1) It is to this very part of the world, specifically Japan, that will serve as the focus of concern in this chapter.

The 16th century ushered in an impressive series of momentous changes in the Western world. For good reason this is called the Renaissance (meaning rebirth) and encompasses the Reformation and Age of Discovery. But what of other corners of the world? What of Japan? Read or reread the appropriate chapter or sections of your textbook to find out. Equally important, how did these two different civilizations respond to one another in perhaps the most dramatic manifestation of the period--exploration and discovery?

Read the document provided carefully. Answer the questions that follow as you attempt to come to terms with cultural transformation.

DOCUMENT

"There are two leaders among the traders, the one called Murashusa, and the other Christian Mota. In their hands they carried something two or three feet long, straight on the outside with a passage inside, and made of a heavy substance. The inner passage runs through it although it is closed at the end. At its side there is an aperture which is the passageway for fire. Its shape defies comparison with anything I know. To use it, fill it with powder and small lead pellets. Set up a small . . . target on a bank. Grip the object in your hand, compose your body, and closing one eye, apply fire to the aperture. Then the pellet hits the target squarely. The explosion is like lightning and the report like thunder. Bystanders must cover their ears. . . . This thing with one blow can smash a mountain of silver and a wall of iron. If one sought to do mischief in another man's domain and he was touched by it, he would lose his life instantly. Needless to say this is also true for the deer and stag that ravage the plants in the fields."

Lord Tokitaka saw it and thought it was the wonder of wonders. He did not know its name at first nor the details of its use. Then someone called it "iron-arms," although it was not known whether the Chinese called it so, or whether it was so called only on our island. Thus, one day, Tokitaka spoke to the two alien leaders through an interpreter: "Incapable though I am, I should like to learn about it." Whereupon, the chiefs answered, also through an interpreter: "If you wish to learn about it, we shall teach you its mysteries." Tokitaka then asked, "What is its secret?" The chief replied: "The secret is to put your mind aright and close one eye." Tokitaka said: "The ancient sages have often taught how to set one's mind aright, and I have learned something of it. If the mind is not set aright, there will be no logic for what we say or do. Thus, I understand what you say about setting our minds aright. However, will it not impair our vision for objects at a distance if we close an eye? Why should we close an eye?" To which the chiefs replied: "That is because concentration is important in everything. When one concentrates, a broad vision is not necessary. To close an eye is not to dim one's eyesight but rather to project one's concentration farther. You should know this." Delighted, Tokitaka said: "That corresponds to what Lao Tzu has said, 'Good sight means seeing what is very small.'"

That year the festival day of the Ninth Month fell on the day of the Metal and the Boar. Thus, one fine morning the weapon was filled with powder and lead pellets, a target was set up more than a hundred paces away, and fire was applied to the weapon. At first the people were astonished; then they became frightened. But in the end they all said in unison: "We should like to learn!" Disregarding the high price of the arms, Tokitaka purchased from the aliens two pieces of the firearms for his family treasure. As for the art of grinding, sifting, and mixing of the powder, Tokitaka let his retainer, Shinokawa Shoshiro, learn it. Tokitaka occupied himself, morning and night, and without rest in handling the arms. As a result, he was able to convert the misses of his early experiments into hits--a hundred hits in a hundred attempts . . . .(2)

QUESTIONS

1. How does Lord Tokitaka respond to his introduction to Western firearms? Is his response favorable, unfavorable, both? Be able to explain and defend your point of view.

2. Check the Endnotes or appropriate section of your textbook to determine who authored the document. Remembering what you learned in an early chapter of this book, Chapter VI, is your interpretation of Lord Tokitaka's response altered? How?

3. Reread the document carefully. Prepare yourself to debate both positions based on the following quote:

    > In short, the major impact of the West on East Asian civilization seems to have been in modern technology and modern forms of organization. Western values such as the importance of the individual have had at best a secondary role. In the sense that modern means have been accepted more readily than traditional Western ends the great transformation of East Asia can be better discribed as "modernization" than as "Westernization."(3)

Endnotes

1.   John K. Fairbank, Edwin O. Reischauer, and Albert M. Craig, <u>A History of East Asian Civilization, Vol. II: East Asia The Modern Transformation</u> (Boston: Houghton Mifflin Company, 1965), 4.

2.   William De Bary, ed., <u>Sources of Japanese Tradition</u> (New York: Columbia University Press, 1958).

3.   Fairbank, Reischauer, and Craig, <u>East Asia The Modern Transformation</u>, 7.

Chapter XII
Looking Twice at the Same Person

The long reign of Louis the XIV (1643-1715) brought to fruition the work of Cardinal Richelieu in his endeavors to strengthen royal power. It was in France, under the rule of the "Sun King," that there emerged a highly developed centralized state. Disorder and insecurity were gradually replaced by religious uniformity, state policy coordinated by mercantilism, and glorification of power. These were the hallmarks of 17th century European civilization and France had one of the most impressive practitioners in Louis.

With dictionary in hand, read through Louis XIV's conception of royal responsibility to his son. Absolutism and skills in reading autobiography are your concern in this important document. Answer each of the questions that follow the document.

DOCUMENT

Two things without doubt were absolutely necessary: very hard work on my part,

and a wise choice of persons capable of seconding it . . . .

I laid a rule on myself to work regularly twice every day, and for two or three hours each time with different persons, without counting the hours which I passed privately and alone, nor the time which I was able to give on particular occasions to any special affairs that might arise. There was no moment when I did not permit people to talk to me about them provided they were urgent . . . .

I cannot tell you what fruit I gathered immediately I had taken this resolution. I felt myself, as it were, uplifted in thought and courage; I found myself quite another man, and with joy reproached myself for having been too long unaware of it. This first timidity, which a little self-judgment always produces and which at the beginning gave me pain, especially on occasions when I had to speak in public, disappeared in no time. The only thing I felt then was that I was King, and born to be one. I experience next a delicious feeling, hard to express, and which you will not know yourself except by tasting it as I have done.

For you must not imagine, my son, that the affairs of State are like some obscure and thorny path of learning, which may possibly have already wearied you, wherein the mind strives to raise itself with effort above its purview, repugnant to us as much as its difficulty. The function of Kings consists principally in allowing good sense to act, which always acts naturally and without effort. What we apply ourselves to is sometimes less difficult than what we do only for our amusement. Its usefulness always follows. A King, however skillful and enlightened be his ministers, cannot put his own hand to the work without its effects being seen. Success, which is agreeable in everything, even in the smallest matters, gratifies us in these as well as in the greatest, and there is no satisfaction to equal that of noting every day some progress in glorious and lofty enterprises, and in the happiness of the people which has been planned and thought out by oneself. All that is most necessary to this work is at the same time agreeable; for, in a word, my son, it is to have one's eyes open to the whole earth; to learn each hour the news concerning every province and every nation, the secrets of every court, the mood and the weaknesses of every Prince and of every foreign minister; to be well-informed on an infinite number of matters about which we are supposed to know nothing; to elicit from our subjects what they hide from us with the greatest care; to discover interests of those who come to us with quite contrary professions. I do not know of any other pleasure we would not renounce for that. . . .

QUESTIONS

1. What particulars does Louis XIV believe are important for his son to rule effectively? How are they representative of the 17th century hallmarks previously articulated?

2. Read through the document again and make a list of what you find admirable about Louis XIV.

3. Read the document for a third time and compile a list of these aspects of Louis you dislike.

4. Compare your two lists and write a two paragraph essay (a biographical vignette) on Louis. Is your vignette well-balanced? Is good biography a balanced presentation? Is real balance possible or does a biographer already have strong opinions about his or her subject? Think about your answer the next time you read a biography.

Endnotes

1. A King's Lessons's in Statecraft: Louis XIV; Letters to His Heirs, Vol. II trans. Herbert Wilson (London: Ernest Benn Limited, 1924), 48-50.

Chapter XIII
The Difficult Art of Biography

Biography is the medium through which the remaining secrets of the famous dead are taken from them and dumped out in full view of the world. The biographer at work, indeed, is like the professional burglar, breaking into a house, rifling through certain drawers that he has good reason to think contain jewelry and money, and triumphantly bearing his loot away. The voyeurism and busy bodyism that impel writers and readers of biography alike are obscured by an apparatus of scholarship designed to give the enterprise an appearance of banklike blandness and solidity. The biographer is portrayed almost as a benefactor. He is seen as sacrificing years of his life to his task, tirelessly sitting in archives and libraries and patiently conducting interviews with witnesses. There is no length he will not go to, and the more his book reflects his industry the more the reader believes that he is having an elevating literary experience rather than simply listening to backstairs gossip and reading other people's mail . . . .(1)

The above thought provoking quote informs you that the focus of this chapter will be biography. In a number of earlier exercises you dealt with issues that touched upon this most difficult genre. Do you remember what they were? It is important for you to do so as a student of history. Ponder this for a moment, for very often when you think of history (other than facts) you think of biography. Famous people are usually the focus and such people have great appeal to us. A number of your exercises in these volumes have centered around famous people for this and other obvious reasons.

Your task will be to learn how to read biography more carefully using the skills from a previous exercise. An ideal opportunity avails you when examining the Enlightenment and enlightened despotism. Of all the interesting enlightened despots--Frederick II of Prussia (1740-86), Joseph II of Austria (1780-90), Gustavus III of Sweden (1771-92)--Sophia Augusta Frederica, better known as Catherine the Great of Russia (1762-96), remains the most intriguing.

Do you remember what enlightened despotism is? Because it remains somewhat difficult to define, here is a review. It evolved out of divine right absolutism embodied best in the person of Louis XIV. But the enlightened despot said little about any divine claim to the throne. Authority was justified on the grounds of usefulness to the state or as Frederick the Great referred to himself, "first servant of the state." With this in mind they built roads, bridges, codified laws, established a professional bureaucracy, repressed localism and provincial autonomy. Owing no special responsibility to either God or church, they favored toleration in religious affairs. They were reformist and rational attempting to implement change through reason, which was to come quickly and was less subject to compromise. As two leading scholars of this period have written, "enlightened despotism . . . was an acceleration of the old institution of monarchy, which now put aside the quasi-sacred mantle in which it had clothed itself and undertook to justify itself in the cold light of reason and secular usefulness . . . ."(2)

Four excerpts follow. They are brief sketches of Catherine the Great. Because few of you will probably be history majors and even fewer professional historians, these vignettes come not from full-length biographies, but instead from assorted texts. Most likely these are the sources where you will encounter Catherine in your studies, so read them carefully as you answer the questions provided you after the documents. By the way, do you know what type of source material you are using?

DOCUMENT 1

Catherine was born as Sophie in 1729 to the ruling family of Anhalt-Zerbst, a small German state on the Baltic. Her education was undistinguished, and her financial and marital prospects were slender. Then in 1744 Empress Elizabeth invited her and her mother to the Russian court. . . . To stabilize Russia's political future, Elizabeth wanted Grand Duke Peter safely married. . . . At the Russian frontier, they were greeted as honored guests of the empress. Rumors spread that Sophie was destined to marry Peter, heir to the throne. Young Sophie, casting her spell over Elizabeth, resolved to remain in Russia. . . . Sophie paid court to Peter, who, by her own account, was ugly, immature, and boastful. She studied Russian assiduously, and won good will at the imperial court. Converted to Orthodoxy "without any effort," she was christened Catherine (Ekaterina Alekseevna) and in 1745 married Peter. Her seventeen-year cohabitation with that perpetual adolescent tested her patience and ambition fully. . . . Soon Paul was born, son of Catherine and probably the courtier Serge Saltykov. Catherine busied herself with amorous adventures, extensive reading, and the study of court politics. She came to the throne as the best-educated, most literate ruler in Russian history. Ambition, vitality, and political shrewdness were her outstanding traits. "I will rule or I shall die," she told the English ambassador in 1757. Frederick II wrote in 1778; "The empress of Russia is very proud, very ambitious, and very vain." Her actions as ruler confirmed the truth of his remarks.(3)

DOCUMENT 2

Shortly after Elizabeth brought Peter to Russia, she also selected for him a wife--Princess Sophia Frederica Augusta of Anhalt- Zerbst, who upon arriving in Russia in 1744, was given the name of Catherine. From inception the marriage was a classic example of incompatibility and infidelity. . . . Catherine . . . was German by birth, French in spirit, Russian and Orthodox by choice, and Machiavellian by training. She was charming, sensual, mature, clever, calculating, deceitful, and had a craving for love and power. . . .

Catherine II became Empress of Russia on July 9, 1762, not by any dynastic claims, nor by a popular revolution, nor by the grace of God, but by means of a successful military coup skillfully engineered by a handful of conspirators with the timely aid of palace guards. To maintain herself in power she condoned the murder of her husband and granted her zealous supporters land, money, and promotions. She forgave or punished lightly her innocent critics, but was brutal in her treatment of those who contemplated replacing her with Ivan VI, who, due to long imprisonment, had been reduced to insanity. . . .

Based on her actions and character she has been termed a dilletante, a hypocrite, an enigma, an enlightened despot, a brilliant adventuress, a reactionary, a glory-seeker, a successful politician, an ambitious opportunist, and a nymphomaniac. She has also been described as a ruler who harvested the seeds of her predecessors, a benevolent despot, a lawgiver, a journalist, a playwright, and an annotator of ancient chronicles. She excelled most, however, as a German who successfully promoted Russia's interests, and particularly, as the extraordinary mistress of twenty-one men.(4)

DOCUMENT 3

With the advent of Catherine II, we come to the most arresting personality to occupy the Russian throne since the death of Peter. Brought up in a petty German court, she found herself transplanted to St. Petersburg as a mere girl, living with a husband she detested, and forced to pick her way through the intrigues that flourished around the Empress Elizabeth. She managed to steer clear of trouble only by using her keen wits. Catherine fancied herself as an intellectual; she wrote plays, edited a satirical journal, and steeped herself in the literature of the Enlightenment. Both before and after ascending the throne she maintained a goodly supply of lovers, several of whom had important roles in affairs of state.(5)

DOCUMENT 4

Sophia Augusta Frederica, better known to history as Catherine the Great, was the daughter of a minor German prince, Christian Augustus of Anhalt-Zerbst. Married to the despicable Tsarevitch Peter III at the age of sixteen, and received into the Orthodox Church under the name of Catherine, this German princess passed several lonely years at the Russian court, where she had few friends and was shamelessly neglected by her husband. She consoled herself with wide reading, learned the Russian language, and identified herself so loyally with the interests of her adopted country . . . . Indiscriminate in her love affairs, and often Machiavellian in her politics, Catherine was none the less a woman of remarkable sagacity and proved an

inspired leader. . . .(6)

QUESTIONS

1. Characterize these portrayals of Catherine the Great. Are they positive; negative; a little of both?

2. Draw some generalizations (remember what these are?) about Catherine based on the four provided sketches. Was she an enlightened despot? What is your evidence?

3. Read each sketch and use subtle doubting; learning something new about someone well-known; and looking twice at the same person. Record your findings.

4. Compare these depictions of Catherine the Great with the other enlightened despots. How much is said about their character; their psychological make-up; their love life? How much do you think this has to do with Catherine's gender? Are powerful women investigated and studied by different standards then powerful men? If so, think about the possible reasons. Curious to test this out? Undertake this same exercise with Elizabeth I of England.

5. Go to your own textbook and see how Catherine has been characterized. How different is it from those sketches provided you in this exercise? Do the times have anything to do with this? Look up the publication dates for all five examples. Have societal changes occurred that might account for these differences? What are they?

Endnotes

1. Janet Malcolm, "The Silent Woman - I," <u>The New Yorker</u>, 23 & 30 August 1993, 86.

2. R. R. Palmer and Joel Colton, <u>A History of the Modern World: To 1815</u>, 4th ed. (New York: Alfred A. Knopf, 1971), 336-37.

3. David MacKenzie and Michael W. Curran, <u>A History of Russia and the Soviet Union</u>, 3rd ed. (Chicago: The Dorsey Press, 1987), 318-319.

4. Basil Dmytryshyn, <u>A History of Russia</u> (Englewood Cliffs, New Jersey: Prentice-Hall, Inc., 1977), 281-84.

5. Crane Brinton, John B. Christopher, and Robert Lee Wolff, <u>A History of Civilization: 1715 to the Present, Vol. II</u>, 3rd ed. (Englewood Cliffs, New Jersey: Prentice-Hall, Inc., 1967), 65.

6. Wallace K. Ferguson and Geoffrey Bruun, <u>A Survey of European Civilization</u>, 3rd ed. (Boston: Houghton Mifflin Company, 1962), 542-43.

DOCUMENTS

Chapter II

The Code of Hammurabi
From Cohn-Haft, Louis, ed., Source Readings in Ancient History, Vol. I: The Ancient Near East and Greece. Copyright (c) 1965 by Macmillan Publishing Company.

Chapter III

The Mahabharata
Excerpt from Sources of Indian Tradition, Stephen Hay, ed. Copyright 1988, (c) Columbia University Press, New York. Reprinted with permission of the publisher.

Chapter IV

The Twelve Tables
From Laws by Cicero, trans. by C. W. Keys. Copyright (c) 1966 by Cambridge University Press. Reprinted by permission of Cambridge University Press.

Chapter V

The Great Learning
Excerpt from Sources of Chinese Tradition by William Theodore De Bary, 1960, (c) Columbia University Press, New York. Reprinted with permission of the publisher.

Chapter VI

Chapter VII

Chapter VIII

Chapter IX

From <u>The Canterbury Tales</u>, by Geoffrey Chaucer, translated by Nevill Coghill. Copyright (c) 1951 by Penguin Classics. Reprinted with permission of Penguin Books, Ltd.

Chapter X

From William H. McNeill and M. R. Waldham, <u>The Islamic World</u>, copyright (c) 1973 by The University of Chicago Press. Used with permission. From <u>The Memoirs of Zehir-ed-Din Muhammed Baber</u>, translated by John Leyden and William Erskine (London: Longman and Cadell, 1826).

Chapter XI

From <u>Sources of Japanese Tradition</u> by William De Bary, 1958, (c) Columbia University Press, New York. Reprinted with permission of the publisher.

Chapter XII

From <u>A King's Lessons in Statecraft: Louis XIV: Letters to His Heirs, Vol. II</u>, trans. by Herbert Wilson. Copyright (c) 1924 Ernest Benn Limited. Reprinted by permission of A & C Black Publishers Limited.

Chapter XIII

From <u>A History of Russia and the Soviet Union</u>, 3rd ed. by David MacKenzie and Michael W. Curren. Copyright (c) 1987 by The Dorsey Press. From <u>A History of Russia</u> by Basil Dmytryshyn. Copyright (c) 1977 Prentice-Hall, Inc. From <u>A History of Civilization: 1715 to the Present, Vol. II</u>, 3rd ed. by Crane Brinton, John B. Christopher, and Robert Lee Wolff. Copyright (c) 1967. Prentice-Hall, Inc. From <u>A Survey of European Civilization</u>, 3rd ed. by Wallace K. Ferguson and Geoffrey Brunn. Copyright (c) 1962. Houghton Mifflin Company. Permission given by the Estate of Geoffrey Brunn.